What others are saying

This book is truly a treasure in the body of Christ. One of the greatest challenges in life for people worldwide, is the quest of knowing one's power spot. Some refer to it as purpose others call it motivation. When you find your "It" you find your purpose, your power and your peace. This is a must read that goes far beyond literary accuracy, this book will launch you into your divine destiny. Don't leave home without It!

—Dr. Patricia Bailey-Lecturer, Author, and Founder of Master's Touch Ministries International.

"What Is It" is a GPS to discovering your true passion, setting goals and fulfilling your dreams. Whether you're on a spiritual, business or personal quest, there is something for you in this awesome book. -Venus Mason Theus, Author of *"Brown Paper Bag,"*

What Is It examines the various ways to discover what our It is and the different ways to help us to get and achieve It now. If you need answers, not sure of your *"It factor"*, or you want to know more about It, this book is a must read.

—Dr. Laureen Wishom, Award-Winning Author of "Fit, Fine & Fabulous in Career, Business & Life"

Rosalind Y. Tompkins's new book, *What Is It,* is personal, practical, powerful and prophetic. This easy yet profound reading material can help one discover, develop and deploy their God given gifts and talents thus fulfilling their highest purpose for which they were born. Others who have obtained their "It" can also be blessed by further impartation and confirmation.

—Dr. Steven Govender

Your *"It"* can be dreams that are imbedded within your DNA that reside deep within your heart. All of us have them, these are thoughts and dreams that may have been lying dormant because of roadblocks along the way such as, low self esteem, and addiction, a bad relationship, a huge disappointment, a financial loss, abuse, health challenges, fear and other things that bind us up in life; but God through Rosalind Y. Tompkins can help your *It* be activated so that you can become a more productive person carrying out your purpose which matches with God's will for your life. I highly recommend *What Is It!*

—Minister Aaronetta Frison

What Is It is an explosive revelatory book for today! The powerful and precise message Rosalind Y. Tompkins so clearly lays out chapter after chapter is encouraging, motivational and refreshing. It is prophetic, directional and teaches you how to navigate your way to having it all. This book, once read, will equip individuals in all walks of life to fulfill purpose, follow dreams, and find what their "It" is. I place it on the top of the "must read list"

—Pastor Darlene Wade

What Is It is a wonderful, moving, and exciting journey that never stops, until you are at the end and then there is more…*Life Lessons*. Rosalind Y. Tompkins does it again. A topic that may sometimes be seen as pedestrian is presented in a light, active, and practical way that can be applied by anyone. *What Is It* is timely, especially in this season of turmoil and uncertainty.

—Richard L. Kwame Lewis

What

is

It?

To Oasis:

What is It?

Blessings!

Rosalind Y. Tompkins

10/16

TATE PUBLISHING
AND ENTERPRISES, LLC

What is it?
Copyright © 2014 by Rosalind Y. Tompkins. All rights reserved.

No part of this publication may be reproduced, stored in a retrieval system or transmitted in any way by any means, electronic, mechanical, photocopy, recording or otherwise without the prior permission of the author except as provided by USA copyright law.

This book is designed to provide accurate and authoritative information with regard to the subject matter covered. This information is given with the understanding that neither the author nor Tate Publishing, LLC is engaged in rendering legal, professional advice. Since the details of your situation are fact dependent, you should additionally seek the services of a competent professional.

The opinions expressed by the author are not necessarily those of Tate Publishing, LLC.

Published by Tate Publishing & Enterprises, LLC
127 E. Trade Center Terrace | Mustang, Oklahoma 73064 USA
1.888.361.9473 | www.tatepublishing.com

Tate Publishing is committed to excellence in the publishing industry. The company reflects the philosophy established by the founders, based on Psalm 68:11,
"The Lord gave the word and great was the company of those who published it."

Book design copyright © 2014 by Tate Publishing, LLC. All rights reserved.
Cover design by Joseph Emnace
Interior design by Jimmy Sevilleno

Published in the United States of America

ISBN: 978-1-63063-895-5
1. Religion / Christian Life / Inspirational
2. Religion / Christian Life / Personal Growth
14.05.22

Dedications

I DEDICATE THIS BOOK to all those who are struggling to find purpose for this season of your life. I also dedicate this book to my family and friends who love me unconditionally.

Acknowledgments

I THANK GOD THE Father, Son, and Holy Spirit for continual guidance and direction. It is he who continues to give me my It and keeps me during all the seasons of my life. I thank God for my husband, Richard Lester Kwame Lewis and my PR Coach, Awesome Pam Perry for all your help and support! I also thank God for those who pray for me daily and helped to birth this book through prayer.

Contents

Introduction	15
What Is It?	19
My Weight Loss It	23
How to Find Your It: Ask	25
How to Find Your It: Get Ready to Seek	29
How to Find Your It: Seek	33
How to Find Your It: Knock	37
Your Riches Are Tied to Your It	41
Doing Whatever it Takes to Get It	45
Harnessing God's Power to Activate Your It	49
Activating the Fruit of the Holy Spirit	53
Love Is a Major Component in Fulfilling Your It	57
You Can Have It	63
Addendum: Life Lessons—Articles from My Community Blog	67
Bibliography	121

Introduction

You Got To Have It

WHAT IS IT that you wakes you up from the inside out?

What is it that screams in silence but comes out as a shout that can only be heard by you and God?

What is it that calls to you when your heart is still and tickles your soul while strengthening your will?

That's the *It* that can be fulfilled when you realize that,
You've got to have your life enhanced;
So take a chance;
To understand that there's more in store;
For those willing to risk it all;

And seek to find what's been left behind
But hidden deep inside.
Come take a ride with me;
Because your journey awaits, your destiny is calling, your purpose is ripe;
So take a bite of the things you desire.
I know you want to go higher and have a ball
Because You've Got to Have *It* & You Can Have *It* All!

I spent twelve years of my life addicted to drugs and alcohol, and believe me it was no picnic. However, I did learn valuable lessons from that experience that I share and examine in all of my books, *As Long As There Is Breath In Your Body, There Is Hope*, *Rare Anointing*, and *You Are Beautiful*.

I must say, through the experience of having been a bonafide drug fiend, I learned what it means to have to have something. When I was addicted to crack-cocaine especially—I learned what it meant to immensely crave something all of the time until I got it. My whole life was consumed with either using, thinking about using, or doing whatever it took to use. I was very passionate about my addiction. Drugs came first period. I had no other choice because I was addicted.

Well it has been over twenty-five years since I have been walking free from drugs and alcohol, and I've come to accept the fact that I have somewhat of an addictive personality. That trait has actually served me well. Over the years, I have learned how to make it work for me because it

WHAT IS IT?

fuels passion and persistence. After getting clean and sober, I had to find another target for all of that energy. I had to find my "it" which I identify as my purpose and destiny. I learned how to use positive passion and persistence to produce life and happiness instead of the death and misery that my addiction to drugs produced.

What is it that distinguishes you from the rest of the world? What is it that whenever you are operating at the top of your game that causes heaven and earth to stand to attention, take notice, and embrace? What is the *It* factor in your life that will cause you to excel and be successful? This book will help you to identify and develop your unique "it" and tap into your personal God-given power so that others will say, "he or she has *it*."

In *What Is It,* we will examine ways to discover what your *It* is and look at ways to help you get *It* now. Ultimately you will see that life is all that it is "cracked-up" to be and dreams do come true when you learn how to define, find, and obtain the *It* for your life.

Now I ask you the question, "What is it that you have got to have?" Not so fast let's get through the clichés and automatic responses. You may say the obvious: food, shelter, clothing, love, sex, belonging, God, etc.—however even after your basic needs are met, there are other personal desires that are imbedded in your DNA that reside deep within your heart. Even after we find God or he finds us, there are still things that are calling us waiting to emerge and be fulfilled. Sometimes they are felt as nagging aches or an itch that needs to be scratched but can't be reached, and that is the *It* that will be revealed as you read this book. In addition, you will also learn ways to fulfill the *It* and live your best life.

What Is It?

WHAT IS IT that causes you to get up in the morning? What is it that causes you to stay up at night? What is it that will not let go of you even after years and years of trying? Whatever that *It* is for you, it is tied to your destiny.

Close your eyes right now. What do you see? Keep looking. What comes into view? Some of you may say there is nothing. Then what do you hear? Listen closely. Do you hear your heart calling to you from deep within? Can you see yourself in a place of true fulfillment and happiness because you are doing what you want to do; you are where you want to be and with whom you want to be with? If not then know that you can. Even if you can see it and hear it already, know that it can become clearer and more focused when you actually obtain it.

The key is in the journey of finding your *It* and the journey begins at birth. The moment you breathe your first breath, you are stepping into the rest of your life. You can spend it chasing your dreams or fulfilling your purpose—only you can make the choice.

We are all born with certain gifts in life. The Bible says to "train up a child in the way he should go and when he is old, he will not depart from it" (Proverbs 22:6 KJV). The way he should go is his or her God-given gifts, talents, and skills. Once parents observe their children, they can determine which way to train or lead them into their destiny. So many times, parents want to raise their children to be *mini-me* when in fact God may have an entirely different plan for their lives. Life truly begins when you find your reasons for living. When you see the vision, write it down and make it plain, that's when you can truly run and ultimately fly into your life's purpose.

The It Factor

The *It* factor is generally thought of as something that makes you stand out in the crowd. Many celebrities, politicians, and movie stars are known for having the *It* factor that causes people to listen to or follow them, thus making them influential and often times very wealthy. Today it is all about how many followers that you have on the social media sites: Twitter, Facebook, LinkedIn and others. While

WHAT IS IT?

this may be one measuring tool that society uses to determine who has that certain *It* factor, this is by no means the measuring tool that we use to determine your God-given *It*. The *It* that I am referring to may not mean that you will have millions of people following you if that is not your God-given purpose. It will mean that when you define, find, and obtain your *It*, you will be able to walk in the *It* factor of your divine destiny and experience all of the perks that go with it such as peace, joy, love, and abundant life.

My Weight Loss It

I WENT THROUGH A very trying time in my life in 2008. I lost my mother to sudden death, I went through a painful divorce, and I lost my job. I also experienced a loss of good health and had to have surgery to remove several fibroid tumors in 2009. I turned to food to comfort me through the tough times, and I began to eat lots of sweets and comfort foods. As a result, I gained weight and before I knew it I was over 200 pounds. That was the largest that I had ever been. I finally decided to do something about it in 2011, and I went back to Jenny Craig Inc. I had a lifetime membership and therefore I decided to go back and give them a try. I was very determined, and my weight loss became my *It* for that season. My desire was to lose the weight that I had gained and maintain a healthy size. In addition to going to Jenny Craig, I joined Gold's

Gym and attended regularly. I put all my focus on losing the weight that I had gained. Even though my metabolism had slowed down tremendously, I kept trying and trying until I eventually lost over thirty pounds and reached my goal. In order to lose the weight, I had to apply the same principles that I outline in *What Is It*. I was so successful at it until my *It* once again led to helping others, and I started working for Jenny Craig as a weight loss consultant for eleven months. During that time, I learned the power of self-control and how vitally important it is in fulfilling your *It*. Often times when life spins out of control, you can gain order and courage by taking control of your life, through pursuing and finding your *It*. We accomplish this by doing whatever it takes to be successful. One way that we can truly be successful is by learning that there is power in giving back what you have been given in order to keep it. I now have a "Losing Weight and Loving Life" group coaching class that meets weekly where I share what I learned as a weight loss consultant and how I am living in order to stay healthy. As a result, I have been able to help hundreds of people lose thousands of pounds and keep them off.

How to Find Your It: Ask

"ASK, AND IT will be given to you; seek, and you will find; knock, and the door will be opened to you: For everyone who asks receives; the one who seeks finds; and to the one who knocks, the door will be opened" Matthew 7:7–8 (NIV).

What are you asking for? Not just with your words but with your heart and soul. Who are you asking to fulfill the request? These are some of the questions that need to first be examined before we can move on. Because it is the recurring themes in our lives that can give us clues as to what the *It* is that we are looking for.

So many times we do not get what we want because we don't know what to ask for or who to ask. To ask simply means to make a request, beg, or desire. In order to determine what to ask for let's look at three things.

1. What do you believe is missing in your life?
2. What have you always wanted to do with your life?
3. What brings you the most joy in your life?

Can you answer those questions without hesitation? If so then you know what your *It* is. If not then begin a time of prayer and listening to hear the answers. Be honest and open in receiving and you might be surprised to learn what your heart is really saying.

Once you determine what you are truly asking for then it is time to determine *who* to ask, in order for it to come to pass. We understand according to the Bible that every good and perfect gift comes from God. What you desire must be something that God can supply. In other words, if it is something destructive, evil, or negative, then you must go back to the drawing board and cleanse your motives. The *why* is just as important as the *what*. If it is just all about you then it is really not your *It* because your *It* is always tied to others. Your reason for living is always greater than yourself. Ask God and wait for the answer. You might say well, "I have asked God and I still don't know." Well don't stop asking until you receive.

Also realize that your *It* changes, evolves, or morphs over the years based upon the seasons of your life. Especially if you are going through times of transition in your life. For example, maybe you have just graduated college, got your first job, started or ended a relationship, had your first child,

WHAT IS IT?

lost a loved one, transitioned from your job, just started a company or ministry, or had your children to grow up and leave home; whatever the transition may be just remember that it is always good to ask several times during your lifespan. Be open to change and please don't get stuck in last season's *It*.

How to Find Your It: Get Ready to Seek

TO SEEK IS to be ever learning and for that to happen you must be like a sponge and not a hard rock. The best case scenario is to be a sponge with a filter because you will not want to take in everything that is poured into you. You will need to filter out the bad and store up the good. Be sure to always leave room for more and be willing to overflow into others. The filter that you need in place is the Holy Spirit of God, who is the spirit of truth. He will lead you and guide you into all truth. You need the Holy Spirit to be the guard of your heart as "out of it are the issues of life." (Proverbs 4:23 KJV)

In order to seek appropriately you must get ready or into position to seek and that includes, *mentally, physically, emotionally,* and *spiritually.*

Mentally—To get into position mentally is to renew your mind daily both in the natural and spiritually speaking. Reading books about your object of desire, attending classes, workshops, webinars, seminars, etc. are what is needed in order to position yourself to hear and receive the understanding and knowledge that it will take to fulfill your life's purpose. Keep your mind sharp by challenging it with math, puzzles, word games, and situations that require you to think. Don't get into a mode or mindset of always asking people what you need to do, or how to do this or that. Figure it out or at least try and don't stop until you have completed your task. Keep your mind sharp by taking vitamins and herbs that help sustain mental clarity and capacity. Exercise also helps with brain functioning. Studies find that those who exercise regularly have a greater capacity for mental sharpness and awareness.

Physically—You will not have the strength to find your *It* if you are sick in your body. Today, we are learning more and more about the importance of exercise and nutrition as it relates to the proper functioning of our bodies. Therefore, it becomes vitally important for us to exercise regularly and eat the proper nutritional vitamin and mineral enriched foods in order to maintain optimum health and weight. Using vitamins and herbs also play major roles in producing good physical health, as do rest and relaxation.

Emotionally—Many times it is in our emotional realm that we are not ready to receive our *It*. When one refuses to grow up emotionally, one tends to operate in childish ways. Instead of forming healthy relationships based upon mutual love and respect, there are game playing and selfishness that result in hurt feelings and stunting of progress and growth. One of the biggest ways that this is played out is in power struggles. Power struggles are those places defined by one person trying to get another person to do something in their way, idea, or methodology. It is often seen in children and parents, and it can lead to some very unhealthy exchanges. These are situations where either the parent or the child is trying to get their way and neither one wants to back down or compromise. Both parent and child are hell bent on getting the other to do what they want. The sad thing is that as parents we should know not to get into power struggles with our children because there is no struggle. We have the power or God given authority as parents to lead. The same thing applies in other relationships where there are power struggles.

When you realize your position or place you can develop true strategies to get your desired outcomes without declaring war and fighting for a position—that either you already have, or you don't truly have the authority to make the call. It is always better to *chill* and *act* not react. That takes emotional maturity which requires growth and transformation. The bible talks about jealousies, divisions, gossiping, etc. as signs of immaturity. When you are jealous and cause strife and quarrel those are sure signs that you are not ready to receive your *It*. But when you begin to allow yourself to find the place of agreement and unite, then those are signs of true growth and emotional well being.

The emotional state that you must seek to always get in and stay in is found in the fruit of the Spirit: love, joy, peace, patience, kindness, goodness, faithfulness, gentleness and self-control. (We will talk more about the fruit of the Spirit in *Activating the Fruit of the Spirit*)

Spiritually—To get in the right position spiritually to define, find, and obtain your *It*, there must first be a personal relationship with God through Jesus Christ, not just church attendance or religious rituals. It is within the context of your relationship with the Lord that you will ultimately seek and find your purpose and destiny, because it is the Lord who predestines you to greatness. It is he that has placed in you the spiritual DNA that you need to succeed.

As a matter of fact your seeking boils down to "seeking first the kingdom of God and His righteousness and all things will be added" (Matthew 6:33 NIV). You may ask, "How do I seek the kingdom of God?" It is a matter of the heart because the kingdom of God resides within the heart. Your heart must be turned towards the Lord through prayer, fasting, reading the Word of God, praising, worshipping, and meditating on the things of God. When you do that you are lining up spiritually with heaven and the Holy Spirit will ultimately be your guide on your journey to find your *It*.

How to Find Your It: Seek

THE JOURNEY IS in seeking and sometimes the answer is the journey. To seek means to search for, to crave, to look for intensely. When you begin seeking, it will take you in all directions and bring you into contact with many different people along the way. Some will help and be positive; others will turn out to be charlatans. I have found that there are primarily four types of people that you will meet on your journey, and they will all be needed in order to help you find your *It*: Givers, Takers, Movers, and Shakers.

Givers—these are the people who have an inherent need to share themselves with others, whether it is time, talent, or money. They do not always share for free but even if there is a fee, you usually receive much more than you pay for. These are people that you need to be on your team.

Be careful not to use or abuse their generosity and learn to become a giver yourself because you cannot give from your heart without receiving much more. Givers add value to your life and journey.

Takers—these are the people who see everyone as an opportunity for them to prosper or get something from. People are not seen as people by takers, they are seen as objects to meet their needs. You will be able to spot a taker by listening to their conversation. They primarily talk to you in such a way as to connect with a need that you have and then promise to help to fulfill that need for a fee. It will always cost you something, and the problem is they do not always deliver.

Which brings me to my next point about takers, they lie. Listen for inconsistencies in their speech and actions. It can be as small as promising to call you when you realize they have a pattern of saying, "I will call you later today." You know that they will not call because that's what they say every time and they do not call. Or as big as taking money from you to perform a service that they cannot, will not, and ultimately do not deliver upon.

Watch out for takers because they can suck you dry and leave you penniless. You will still be seeking but now you will have fewer resources to obtain your goals. While takers devalue your life and journey, you will still need them in order to learn valuable lessons about who not to trust and what not to do.

Movers—Movers are those who God has given authority and power to influence others on your behalf. Movers are few and far between because everyone that has the power to influence on your behalf may not. However, the movers that are sent to you on your journey will use their influence for your good. You can target movers to help but most come by serendipity. You just happen upon them. That is why positioning is so important because you are not seeking people but you are seeking God. As you follow the leading of the Holy Spirit, you will find yourself in the right place at the right time. Movers definitely add value to your life.

Shakers—Shakers are those who God allow in your life to keep you on your toes because shakers have a knack for causing angst. They like to keep a lot of drama going on, and shakers tend to always have issues with some aspect of life, and if they are a part of your journey, you may find yourself in the middle of crisis after crisis with shakers. These are the people that you will spend time praying for and about. They will keep you humble and on your knees.

We generally don't like the shakers, but they do indeed bring change. God often uses them to help course correct when we are going in the wrong direction. Shakers can add value or devalue your life depending upon your response. If you allow yourself to learn from each situation that you face with a shaker then it can facilitate your growth and development, however if you allow the shakers to become stumbling blocks then you can get stuck in turmoil, petty mess, and circumstances. In the long run, you must learn to keep a cool head with shakers around. Don't get angry or bitter.

The key to navigating and finding your *It* remains in seeking the Lord for direction no matter if you happen to be surrounded by Givers, Takers, Movers, or Shakers.

How to Find Your It: Knock

TO KNOCK MEANS to strike something with a sharp blow, to collide with something, to make a pounding noise, to set forcibly in motion with a blow. You are not going to find your *It* by being timid and afraid. You must strike out and that denotes passion. You must be passionate about getting what you need and desire because if you are not passionate about it then no one else will be.

I have met many people who wanted to step out and take the journey to find their true purpose in life; however they did not have the gusto to do it. What I mean is they lacked the force that is needed to thrust them into their destiny. "The Kingdom of Heaven suffers violence but the violent take it by force" (Matthew 11:12 NKJV). You can receive the force that you need by knocking correctly.

First of all knocking requires persistent striking. Do not give up after the first try, continue to try and try again, until you get an answer. Even after you get an answer if it is not the desired yes then ask the same question in a different way. You will be surprised to see the positive results that you will achieve just by your persistence.

The next thing that you must understand about knocking is where to knock. In other words you don't want to waste your time asking the wrong source for your desired answer. For example you can knock all day long at the gas station but if you need fish for dinner, even after they open the door you will not get what you need. So make sure if you need fish you are knocking on the fish market's door.

Lastly to knock requires strength because you are exerting energy. So many times we don't knock because we lack the strength to do so. Primarily the strength should come from God and not just you. In other words you need to knock with supernatural force in order to get some doors open. You need God's power to keep up the pace and persistence. That power is accessed through prayer and fasting. It is also released through praise and worship—for more details, you can check the chapter entitled "Harnessing God's Power." Just remember you don't have to knock in your own strength. It is God who will ultimately open the door anyway because whatever door he opens no man can close and whatever door he closes no man can open.

Some may ask "Well, if it is God who does all the work, then why do I have to do anything?" The answer is faith without works is dead. We are partners and co-laborers with God. It is not about us just believing but we must do our part. We are God's hands, feet, legs, mouth, etc. We are the body of Christ so we must move in order to function properly. When you sit back and wait on God to do everything for you just because you "prayed about it," then you are wasting precious time and energy, and you will never obtain your *It* or true purpose and destiny in life.

Your *It* is waiting for you to ask, seek, and knock.

Your Riches Are Tied to Your It

ARE YOU MAKING a living by doing what you always wanted to do? Is your chosen profession bringing you pleasure? Would you do the work that you are doing now for free? Do you realize that you can live a life where your answers to all of the proposed questions are yes? You can when your *It* is leading your riches and not your riches leading you. One of the reasons that finding your *It* is so important is because your *It* is directly associated with the riches that are just waiting to be yours.

So many times we get involved in get rich quick schemes and ventures just to make money so we can live life on our terms. The problem is when the scheme or venture or even a job or profession does not line up with the internal and eternal plans designed by God for our lives; we can began to feel out of synch, and even though we may be making a living there is a longing for more.

You want more time to explore and have fun doing what you desire not just what is required.

In order for your riches to come from finding and fulfilling your *It* or personal purpose and destiny in life, you must not compromise. You must forsake all things that clutter your life and that are not tied to your *It*. That may sound difficult but if you try to hold on to things that pull you further away from your desired goals then you will be torn, split, and miserable. Just remember as it says in the word of God, "You cannot serve two masters."

We are all born with gifts and talents that make us unique. Your greatest treasures reside on the inside of you not the outside. They are very valuable to others once you understand what they are and how to give them to the people that they were put inside of you for. That may sound strange when we are talking about getting riches; however you must learn to give in order to receive. When you begin to give of your God given talents and gifts your riches will appear.

They will come from people who find what you have to give to be valuable and precious. It is very important how you carry, package, and market your *It*. You have to believe in your own inherent abilities and value in order for others to believe in you.

I learned this lesson early in my career as a gospel preacher. I'll share the following real-life incident that happened to me to help illustrate this point. I was one of seven speakers at a church service about the fruit of the Spirit. We each had to talk about one or two characteristics and I was given joy. I remember that it was getting very late that night, and I was the last speaker to get up. By the time I was called up to share, most people were tired and ready to go home. Everyone had pretty much said everything that could be said about the subject. I got up and began to talk about how we must kick the devil out of our lives in order to have joy, and I gave a demonstration. Well, as I lifted my leg to kick in the very long dress that I was wearing, I ended up losing my balance and falling flat on my behind. The crowd woke up then and began to laugh.

I jumped up and kept sharing my message and told them that I was glad that they had joy then because they looked like they were sucking on lemons before. That service was a defining moment in my preaching and speaking career. I could have easily given up and never preached again because it was a very humiliating experience. However, I knew that speaking was a part of my *It*, and I believed in my ability to preach. I understood that there would be challenges that I would have to overcome, and I decided that night not to take myself too seriously and to continue on no matter what. I learned that the primary way that you showcase your power is by keeping it positive. A good sense of humor and a positive attitude will tremendously increase your earning potential and help you to obtain your *It*.

Doing Whatever it Takes to Get It

I STARTED USING MARIJUANA when I was twelve-years old, and I was a drug addict for twelve years of my life. I was snorting cocaine by the time I was seventeen-years old. I had broken with reality and having psychotic episodes as a result of using hallucinogenic drugs around the age of nineteen resulting in multiple psychiatric hospitalizations. God miraculously healed my mind, but at the age of twenty-one I was introduced to crack-cocaine.

My whole life changed when I started using crack because all of a sudden I could no longer function in normal society. For the second time in my drug-using history, I could not go to school while using, I couldn't study, work, or do anything positive. I had finally met my match.

You might say that I was a functional addict prior to crack because even though I used some type of drug every day, I still went to college and made decent grades. I even worked different jobs and did my internship, but with crack it was different.

Being a crack addict was even worse than the psychotic episodes that I had experienced, because while on crack I was cognizant enough to think about using and doing whatever it took to use. When I had broken with reality from using the psychedelic drugs, I didn't think about using I was somewhere in la-la land. I *thank* God for deliverance. I have also shared in detail about my addiction and recovery in my first book *As Long As There Is Breath in Your Body, There Is Hope*.

Crack-cocaine addiction consumed my life. If I wasn't using, I was thinking about using to the point of being physically sick. I couldn't sleep or eat. I would just lay in my bed staring at the ceiling aching all over as my brain worked overtime trying to come up with schemes to get more drugs. I had to have it, not getting it was simply not an option. I needed it to survive, to feel normal, and to live. Therefore, I understand very well the concept of wanting something so badly until you are willing to do whatever it takes to get it. It takes a great amount of passion and boldness to live like that. There has to be an inner drive that is continuing to thrust you forward.

WHAT IS IT?

Once I got free from addiction to drugs and alcohol, I began to feel a void in my life. I couldn't quite put my finger on what it was. I was living my life one day at a time enjoying my sobriety. I was a Christian with a strong foundation and faith in God. I was the single parent of a beautiful baby girl. I had finished my degree, and I had started a great social work career—but something was missing. It wasn't until I got the vision from the Lord to start the non-profit ministry, Mothers In Crisis, Inc., that I understood what I needed in my life. You see I was missing *It*.

Yes, everything that I was doing was a part of my purpose, but my *It* for that season was the thing that would pull everything together and fill the void that was still there.

Once I embarked on the quest to start Mothers In Crisis, I found that I was either doing the work of helping others to get free of drugs and alcohol addiction or thinking and praying about things that we could do to help others and the organization. Believe me, I was willing to do whatever it took and I did. I started the organization and successfully managed the operation through grant writing and administrative work as well as providing direct services for over two decades, and as a result Mothers In Crisis helped over ten-thousand families live drug-free productive lives. I give God all the glory. I share this to illustrate the type of commitment and passion that you must have in order to find and fulfill your *It*.

For this season of my life, I am currently seeking, finding, and implementing my next *It*, Hope Universe, the next chapter of Mothers In Crisis. I am on assignment to help spread hope around the world. Why don't you join me and become a Citizen of Hope Universe because citizenship does have privileges. For more information, please visit the website: www.Hope-Universe.com. This time it is different than before but the principles are the same. I must use the same persistence and passion in order to bring it to fruition. In order to obtain your *It*, remember:

- Don't settle for the status quo.
- Spend time everyday either seeking, finding, or implementing your *It*.
- Be willing to pay the cost or sacrifice that it is going to take because it is going to cost you.

Harnessing God's Power to Activate Your It

GOD'S POWER IS the precious commodity that is needed to fuel your passion, and it is also needed to activate your purpose. I liken this power to the renewable energy sources that governments, corporations, and other organizations are looking for ways to harness in order to lessen dependence on traditional fuel supplies. The unique thing about renewable energy sources is that they are energy sources that are continually replenished. These include energy from water, wind, the sun, geothermal sources, and biomass sources such as energy crops. In contrast, fuels such as coal, oil, and natural gas are nonrenewable. Once a deposit of these fuels is depleted it cannot be replenished. A replacement deposit must be found instead. Both renewable and non-renewable energy sources are used to generate electricity, power vehicles, and provide heating, cooling, and light. Although water, wind, and other renewable sources may appear free, their cost comes in collecting, harnessing, and transporting the energy so that it can do useful work. Just as there are costs associated with harnessing renewable energy sources; there are costs associated with harnessing God's power when finding your *It*. Those costs are time, sacrifice, and obedience.

Let's look at how time, sacrifice and obedience are needed when receiving God's power. Time is needed because you must wait or tarry on the Lord until the appointed time comes to receive the promise of God through the Holy Spirit. Time is also needed to produce the all important fruit of God's spirit. Sacrifice is needed because you will be required to give up some things that may be harmful distractions to your God given purpose. Obedience is needed because you must do what the Lord instructs you to do in order to receive his power.

In Acts 1:8 in the Bible, Jesus tells his disciples that after the Holy Spirit comes upon them they shall receive power. In Acts 2, we see the power of God manifested on the day of Pentecost when the disciples and others received an outpouring of God's spirit. That outpouring established the early church, and they were able to harness God's power to preach the gospel, heal the sick, cast out devils and advance the kingdom of God.

WHAT IS IT?

Today we too must receive the power of the Holy Spirit in order to successfully seek, find, and implement our *It*. One way to harness the Holy Spirit's power is through understanding the fruit of the Holy Spirit and knowing how to activate it.

Activating the Fruit of the Holy Spirit

ACCORDING TO THE Bible the fruit of the Spirit is love, joy, peace, patience, kindness, goodness, faithfulness, gentleness, and self-control. The fruit represents the character of God that is grown, processed, and developed in the soul and heart. It is power that is produced through time, sacrifice, and obedience to Christ and his Word.

In order to activate the fruit of the Holy Spirit to help in your quest to seek, find, and fulfill your *It*, there has to be agreement, unity, and harmony in your life. Agreement, unity, and harmony are the atmospheric conditions needed to produce the fruit of the Spirit. That is what releases the power to be successful. Where there are divisions, disagreements, offenses, strife, and all forms of negativity, there is negative power released to destroy not build; to kill not heal; and to steal not grow.

Whenever you are ready to fulfill your purpose on planet earth find others who will agree with you and be willing to support you. Whether it is financial, emotional, spiritual, etc., it is very important to have agreement. It doesn't have to be a crowd either, one or two people are all you need. However, it needs to be true heart agreement and not just words. Some people will tell you that they are with you but when it comes time to actually help you they won't. Some people will actually talk against what you are doing so be careful who you share your *It* with. Where there is true agreement there is power. True agreement will lead to unity and where there is unity God commands his blessings. You are definitely going to need God's blessings in order to accomplish your goals. Harmony is manifested when you can flow together with others as you step into your greatness. So many times we want to be one man or one woman shows but what we really need is to find the people that we can harmonize our lives with much like the birds, squirrels, honey bees, trees, rabbits, water streams, and all the creatures and things of nature. Nature gives us a beautiful picture of what it means to be in harmony.

Spiritual It Factor Scale

The *It* Factor Scale is based upon the Nine Fruit of the Spirit as found in (Galatians 5:22 –23 NIV). The *It* Factor Scale is designed to rate your ability to become aware, grow, activate, and live a fruitful life filled with the Holy Spirit.

On a scale from one to ten—one (1) being the least and ten (10) being the greatest. Rate your level for each characteristic and afterwards add your score. Top score available is Ninety (90).

Circle your number for each characteristic and add score for each day. I suggest measuring your Spiritual *It* Factor periodically to see where you are.

Love

1   2   3   4   5   6   7   8   9   10

Joy

1   2   3   4   5   6   7   8   9   10

Peace

1   2   3   4   5   6   7   8   9   10

Patience

1   2   3   4   5   6   7   8   9   10

Kindness

1   2   3   4   5   6   7   8   9   10

Goodness

1   2   3   4   5   6   7   8   9   10

Faithfulness

1   2   3   4   5   6   7   8   9   10

Gentleness

1   2   3   4   5   6   7   8   9   10

Self-Control

1   2   3   4   5   6   7   8   9   10

Scoring

90   You are living a Fruitful, Spirit Filled Life
70–90   The Fruit of the Spirit is alive and active in your life
50–70   You are growing in the Fruit of the Spirit
30–50   You are beginning to activate the Fruit of the Spirit
09–30   You are aware of the Fruit of the Spirit

Love Is a Major Component in Fulfilling Your It

THERE IS NO power greater than love and in order to be successful in seeking, finding, and fulfilling your *It* you must learn how to love and to be loved. Love is a topic that has been written about and contemplated throughout the ages since the beginning of time. Families have been formed and divided all in the name of love. Yet people continue to ask "What is love?" and in some cases, "What's love got to do with it?" When it comes to fulfilling your *It*, love has everything to do with it.

According to scriptures in the Bible, God is love and love is patient, kind, keeps no records of wrongs, covers faults, and never fails; but wars have been fought all in the name of love. In contrast to the biblical view, society's definitions of love are often based upon common myths about love that we see in Hollywood movies or romance novels. They portray love in a cookie cutter fashion in which boy meets girl, and they "fall in love" and experience conflict but ultimately get together and live happily ever after. While we may know that in most cases this is a fantasy; somewhere deep inside we look for that kind of love and oftentimes judge the love that we have because it doesn't look like what is portrayed in the movies as the ideal love.

My definition of love has evolved over the years based upon my experiences and my beliefs. I am a woman who loves deeply, and I have literally loved people back to life through my ministries of Mothers In Crisis and Turning Point International Church. I am capable of making deep connections with others that are based upon the concepts of mutual love and respect. In addition to all of that and most importantly, I experienced the love of Christ firsthand when I went through my drug addiction and other trying periods in my life.

Over the years, I have found that the best way to really experience love is moment by moment. My personal definition of love, in addition to what the Bible says, is strong feelings and pleasurable emotional connections with others that elicit positive thoughts and actions designed to interpret, enjoy, reciprocate and express the experiences. This love can be found in long-term monogamous marital relationships as well as familial, friendship, and other relation-

WHAT IS IT?

ships where two people connect for purpose and destiny to be revealed and fulfilled.

I believe that there are opportunities to love all around you everyday, and when you see that you will realize that you are blessed beyond measure. Just because you may not be experiencing the traditional type of love within a marriage, you do have the capacity to embrace the moments of love that are available to you. Embracing moments of love will give you the power, zeal, and energy needed to seek, find, and fulfill your *It*.

Moments of love can occur within the context of interactions in relationships where bonding takes place and the hormone oxytocin is released. Oxytocin has been nicknamed by some the "cuddle hormone" or the "love hormone," but it actually acts within the body and the brain. Oxytocin plays a key role in social bonding and attachment. Although oxytocin is released in humans during sexual intercourse for men and women and during childbirth and lactation for women; oxyctocin is also released during everyday activities and interactions where bonding takes place such as playing with your children, meeting and getting to know new people, during successful business deals with new partners, and hanging out with family and friends. Studies show that through oxytocin surges trust and cooperation are greatly increased. In other words, we are wired to love. Oftentimes we miss out on the opportunities to enjoy our love connections because they don't fit the mold of what we believe love should look like. I have experienced love during times of praise and worship, prayer and meditation, both at church with others and alone in my prayer closet. I have experienced these moments of love with family, friends, and loved ones. Since I have become aware of the power of these moments of love, I experience them more deliberately and more often. I have come to realize that love is a major component in fulfilling your *It*.

Loving Your Enemies

One of the reasons that love is such a powerful force is because it cancels out the negativity that comes against you once you begin to define, find, and obtain your *It*. I made the mistake of believing that people were going to be happy about me, stepping into a place of divine order and grace for my life when I first started walking in my *It*, but I soon realized that there were those who immediately opposed the good that I was trying to do. Although I was stunned, I realized that jealousy and envy are real issues that many people struggle with. When some people see you succeeding; they are immediately confronted with their own shortcomings and instead of applauding your process and progress, they try to hinder you.

The only way to successfully deal with the *haters* is through love. When you make up in your mind that you will not allow the poison of unforgiveness, bitterness, hatred, and resentment to enter into your life and heart; you can continue to pursue your purpose and fulfill your destiny. I've found that praying for those who are against you and distancing them in your heart and life so they will not be able to hurt you, are two surefire ways to love your enemies.

You Can Have It

OKAY NOW, LET'S summarize what you need to know in order to define, find, and obtain your *It*.

- Your *It* is your personal purpose and destiny in life, your mission or reason for living.
- You are born with certain God given gifts and talents that are tied to your *It*.
- Your *It* can change or morph from season to season but the basic foundation will remain the same.
- When life spins out of control, you can gain order and courage by taking control of your life, through pursuing and finding your *It*.

- There is power in giving back what you have been given in order to keep *It*.
- You must *ask*, *seek*, *knock* in order to find your *It*.
- You must be passionate and persistent about pursuing and fulfilling your *It*.
- Your riches are tied to your *It*.
- You have to be willing to do what it takes to get your *It*.
- You need to harness God's Power to get your *It*.
- Time, sacrifice, and obedience are needed when receiving God's power for your *It*.
- In order to activate the fruit of the Holy Spirit to help in your quest to seek, find, and fulfill your *It*, there has to be agreement, unity, and harmony in your life.
- There is no power greater than love and embracing moments of love will give you the power, zeal, and energy needed to seek, find, and fulfill your *It*. When you make up in your mind that you will not allow the poison of unforgiveness, bitterness, hatred, and resentment to enter into your life and heart; you can continue to pursue your purpose and fulfill your destiny.

WHAT IS IT?

The good news is that you can have *It*. Everything that belongs to you can be yours if you don't give up, trust God, and apply these principles.

Addendum: Life Lessons—Articles from My Community Blog

NOW THAT YOU have been equipped to take the dip and walk in your purpose and destiny, I will provide additional bonus material in this last chapter. I have found that during seasons of transition it is very helpful to be coached or mentored by people who have gone through the same or similar life events. I've been coached by great people whose expertise and life lessons helped me to navigate through tough seasons of my life. I am also a life coach who helps people to release their greatness from within. One of the ways that I coach is through writing a blog. For the remainder of the book, I will share articles from my blog for my local newspaper, *The Tallahassee Democrat* that contain real life lessons that I have learned. These life lessons can give you valuable information that will also help you to define, find, and obtain your *It* for this season of your life.

Life Lesson: Am I really free?

"If I am free and my brothers and sisters are not; then am I really free?" Many memories flooded my mind as I sat on the stage waiting to receive my doctorate in humanities that was being conferred upon me by Dr. Gregory Wright, founder, president, chancellor of the Five-Fold Ministry Theological University out of San Diego, California. It was indeed an honor to be recognized as a humanitarian after two decades of service to mankind through Mothers In Crisis. After impacting the lives of over ten-thousand families and sacrificing much, I was now officially in the ranks of many of my heroes such as Martin Luther King, Jr., Mother Theresa, Oprah Winfrey, Mahatma Gandhi, Reverend Jesse Jackson, and even Michelle Obama.

I don't often think in details about the past in terms of what I went through during my addiction because it has been over twenty-five years since I have been clean but this night brought back so many memories. I might add that many of which are found in my first book, *As Long As There*

WHAT IS IT?

Is Breath In Your Body, There Is Hope. I did not have a speech prepared but I knew that I would be called upon to give an acceptance speech. I thought I would just say thanks and give glory to God; but when I stood behind the podium and opened my mouth, the first thing that came out was how I lost my first daughter. She was stillborn because of my drug addiction. I carried her for six months and then she stopped breathing. Needless to say the tears began right then and continued throughout my talk.

I found myself speaking of the broken moments in my life and ministry. I thought this was profound because it is in the broken places that we are certified to be used. I did not stand in "pomp and circumstance," but I stood in humility and brokenness as I shared from my heart. At one point, I made the statement above which has been a driving force throughout my career, "If I am free but my brothers and sisters are not; then am I really free?" The answer for me has always been "*no!*" That is why I did not opt to get a nice paying job, go back to school, and forget about what I had been through. I couldn't and I am finding that even now—I can't.

I am indeed a humanitarian and a freedom maker because I will not stop trying to relieve the pain and suffering of mankind in any way that I possibly can—whether it is from the small cubicle that I occupy as a weight-loss consultant at Jenny Craig, or from the pulpit that I occupy as senior pastor at Turning Point International Church.

Life Lesson:
Stop the Violence, Please?

I received a call last week from one of my church members who was frantically looking for her husband to tell him his daughter, by his first wife, had just gotten shot. She asked me to please be praying. I immediately thought about the ages of his daughters, fifteen- and seventeen-years old, and I wondered, how in the world did that happen, and which one had been shot? I said, "Shot, how, what, when, where?" all in one breath. My mind flashed back to these teenagers who came to church from time to time with their father and frequented their mother's church quite often. I knew them to be kind and beautiful girls with typical teenage problems but nothing out of the ordinary. They were not known gang members or prone to violence like I was at their age, but that is another story.

I was told that they did not have all the details, but it appeared to be a drive by shooting on the Southside of town, and the girls just happened to be in the wrong place at the wrong time. When I got off the phone I immediately called a prayer partner and we begin to pray. Soon after the father called and said they were on the way to the hospital and to please keep his daughter in prayer because the bullet was traveling through her back, and they didn't know where it would end up. It was a very critical situation. I later found out the details of the shooting, and it was extremely ran-

WHAT IS IT?

dom indeed. It could have happened to anyone and it could have been an instant tragedy ending in death.

The two sisters had gone school shopping, and they were driving home on South Meridian when they came upon a shoot-out between two men. One of the men ran in front of the car and the seventeen-year-old, who was driving, stopped the car to keep from hitting him. The other man kept on shooting and a bullet hit the hood of the steel car and bounced off the windshield and entered through the glove compartment. The bullet hit the fifteen-year-old who was sitting in the front passenger seat in the right shoulder area. She immediately slumped over, and her sister drove them to get help.

The bullet eventually lodged in her right lung causing no major damage. Even the doctor said that it was only the grace of God that it did not hit her heart, a major artery, or spinal cord. They could not operate because of where it is, but they hope that it will eventually pass out of her body naturally. She is now home from the hospital recovering; she has nightmares and is having difficulty breathing. I asked her father what can we do and are they in need of anything? He said please tell people to pray for my daughter and our family.

Listed below are things that we can do to stop the violence. Please note that some are contradictory in nature but I included them because they are being discussed as credible options.

- It starts with education. We must educate our families and communities about the issues surrounding violence highlighting ways to handle conflict. We must also talk about safety measures and precautions.

- Gun control is needed to limit the amount of guns available to people who may use them to harm others, especially certain types of guns and weaponry that is considered extremely dangerous and unnecessary for civilian use.

- More compassion is needed with greater respect and niceness among people.

- More guns and less control are needed for citizens to be able to protect themselves from potential killers.

- We need to have dialogue and ongoing discussions about violence prevention as a part of our local and national agenda not just when tragedy strikes but all the time.

- There is a need for profiles to be developed with ways to identify potentially violent prone individuals. There is also a need for strategies to help these individuals and prevent them from tipping over the edge.

- We need to pray for our families, communities, nation, and world.

Life Lesson: In Times of Transition

The definition of transition is movement, passage, or change from one position, state, stage, subject, concept, etc., to another; change, and truth be told we all are experiencing some degree of change at all times. Some to a greater extent than others I must say, but we are all experiencing change. We can look at the four seasons of weather: summer, fall, Winter, and Spring, and realize nothing remains the same.

The problem with change is oftentimes the transitioning from one state to the other is off. Using the weather example, if it is winter and you are still living as though it is summer, you will have a hard time keeping warm. This often happens when we do not experience fall correctly. In other words I see fall as a transitioning Season. It is a time when we begin to see the color of the leaves changing on the trees and the weather getting cooler in the evenings and in the mornings. This gives us an opportunity to prepare for the winter months that are coming by pulling out the warmer clothes, and preparing our heating equipment, etc. If we ignore the signs of fall, it does not stop winter from appearing; it just makes us ill-prepared to deal with it.

In times of transition, it is important to remember that while transitioning is often designed to help us to navigate to the next phase much like labor is to delivery, it is also a time of great opportunity to grow and develop. It is not a time to close our eyes and hope it ends soon, but it is a time to open our eyes and hearts to the beauty of what is happening. We can learn great life lessons in times of transition.

Some transitions last hours while others take years. When the transition takes longer, you may have a tendency to want to stay in the place of transition but don't get comfortable and build a nest because that will hinder your ability to move to the desired place, state, position, etc. You must also remember that some of the people that are with you during the transition are there for a season and a reason and when the time is up, you must let them go.

I like many others are going through times of transition during this season and sometimes it feels like "this is it," this is the way it is and will always be. And other times, it feels as though I am just passing through as a nomad, looking for a place to land and call my own. No matter how I feel at any given time, it always helps to hold on to familiar and stable places in my mind, heart, spirit, and soul. These are the places where love lives. For me they are faith, family, friends, freedom, and fun! No matter what is going on in my life I hold these places near and dear to my heart, and it anchors me for whatever is happening to me or around me. I know when it is all said and done these are the things that I will always carry with me. You see, there are some places that you must never allow to move too far from you no matter what time or season it may be in your life—"A time to weep and a time to laugh; A time to mourn and a time to dance" (Ecclesiastes 3:4 kjv).

Life Lesson: Here Just Taking Up Space

I had a conversation with a young lady the other day that was going through some pretty tough situations in her life, and I asked her did she know why she was here. She looked at me and said, "Do you mean right here in this room?" I said to her, "No on planet earth, why are you here?" She thought for a while and then said five words that shook me to my core, and those were "I'm here just taking up space."

I knew immediately that all the things that were happening in her life were a result of the fact that she had no conscious purpose for living. She was living her life on automatic pilot just doing what was required of her and stumbling and falling along the way as she searched for meaning.

How many of us live our lives that way, not really aware and awake to the things that are significant but just doing what is required for survival? It doesn't matter how young or how old you are because I have talked to people in their early twenties and those in their eighties who simply do not know why they are here. They truly believe that they are here just taking up space.

I wrote a poem a few years ago entitled "Dream Again" and one part goes like this—

> for the first time in my life my eyes were wide open and I was aware and awake to the things that make life worth living and time worth giving, to the things that bring relief and offer peace.
>
> This poem is taken from my book, *You Are Beautiful*.

I was referring to purpose. Whenever we know our purpose for living, giving, loving, being, and breathing, we enter a life that is focused and meaningful. Even through the rough and tough terrain of life, we are able to continue when we know why we are here.

As a matter of fact, your life's mission and vision are developed based upon why you are here. Everything flows from the place of purpose. When you know your purpose you can ask the question at any given time, "Is what I'm doing right now a part of the master plan for my life?" In other words, "Does it fit into the patterns of my existence and if it does not then why am I doing it?"

None of us are here just taking up space, we all have something to do and contribute to the great scheme of things we call life. It is our mission to find and fulfill that purpose every day because it can change along the way. It has to because we are always growing and changing.

WHAT IS IT?

The last part of the poem, "Dream Again" says in the following passage:

> Whether awake or asleep, dream of a life filled with songs for the soul and love that makes whole, whatever is broken. Dream of hope and joy for better days ahead and when you dream get out of your bed, and bring to reality the things that were said!
>
> This poem is taken from my book, *You Are Beautiful..*

Life Lesson: Letting go of the Past and Embracing the Future

One of my mentors—a dear elderly woman who has since passed—once said to me, "Rosalind, you have to wear people like loose clothing." When I asked her what she meant by that she said, "You have to be ready to shed them when needed." I remember thinking that was pretty cynical but today, many years later, I can understand what she was saying to me. I have come to realize that people come into your life for a reason and for a season. I found this to be especially true with the death of my mother four years ago. She was in my life for forty-plus years, and when it was time for her to go I had no choice but to let her.

Because of the finality of it, death is a perfect example of letting go. Let us apply the concept of death to other areas where things are done and over with such as our past. Whether good or bad, it is over—never to be lived again. That includes relationships, jobs, even our lives because we will never be the age that we were years ago.

I believe the greatest problem that we have with letting go of the past is fear of the future. The unknown, the unfamiliar, the uncharted territories often bring tremendous anxiety. It is sometimes easier to remember how we used to be, what we used to do, how we used to feel, what we used to have and spend most of our days so caught up in yesterday until today is gone and tomorrow is never considered.

Letting go of the past can only truly be accomplished when we embrace the future. It's like having gold in your hand and not wanting to let it go. If you hold on to it that is all you will have, but if you let go of it more can come in. If you open up to the present and embrace the future, you will have so much more. If the past is good, you will always have those good memories to treasure. If it is not so good, you can always remember but not let past events traumatize you. This can be done by embracing the possibilities of what is to come and not just dwelling on what has been.

Here are three ways that have helped me to let go of the past and embrace the future:

1. I learned the power of possibility thinking.
2. I imagine my life as I want it to be not as it is or was.

3. I speak words of potential and power over my future—for example: "I will succeed, failure is not an option".

Life Lesson: I Believe in You

We often spend so much time invested in making money but what if we spent that time invested in making people. One great way that we can do that is to look for the best in others and when we find it make sure they see it. "It takes two to know one." We cannot see ourselves by ourselves and therefore we need others in our lives that can genuinely see us. I believe in you because that helps me to believe in myself. If I can see the greatness in you then I know there has to be greatness in me to be able to identify it in others.

Five steps to positively instill Belief

1. Begin to really look at the people in your life, at home, school, work, the community and identify their strengths and not just their weaknesses.
2. Build strong relationships based upon mutual love and respect with them.
3. Tell them the positive attributes that you see in them.
4. In word and deed say to them, "*I believe in you!*"

5. Don't stop encouraging them in what you see until they see and believe it too.

Life Lesson: The Truth of it All

I believe that we will all breathe a collective sigh of relief when this political season is over. Lately everywhere I go there seems to be a resounding theme to the conversations surrounding politics. Whether it is found in the polite whispers of those who still believe that politics and religion are taboo topics in public places or those who proudly wear buttons with their candidate's face smiling at you and thus shouting their political beliefs. I keep hearing people say *"I wish they would just tell the truth!"*

There are so many lies swirling around the atmosphere until one could literally drown in the emissions of hot air. I don't know if it is because today we have so many "fact checkers" that can give us the truth in real time via the internet and social media or if people are now becoming more savvy when it comes to political rhetoric, but it seems as though lies are becoming the political norm. Whatever happened to the days when President George Washington's famous quote, *"I cannot tell a lie"* was the rallying cry? Now it appears as though *"I cannot tell the truth"* is the order of the day.

WHAT IS IT?

The truth of the matter is that we all have our personal truths based upon our experiences which become our stories. Our stories help to mold and shape us whether good or bad. When we tap into the truth of what we tell ourselves about ourselves we can live authentic lives. It becomes increasingly difficult to be authentic in a society that accepts lies as a normal part of the political process. If we allow our leaders to do it on both sides of the aisles then we are silently saying that it is okay for us to believe and speak lies about ourselves and others in order to "win" in life.

Truth is subjective based upon personal beliefs, but facts are objective based upon actual events. We can find harmony when the two agree. When our truths line-up with the actual facts of our lives, then we can become authentic in our thinking and living. I have found that while this sounds easy, it is very hard to put into practice because sometimes the truth is hard to swallow; but just like my mother always told me about castor oil, *"It may not taste good to you, but it is good for you!"*

No matter how many untruths, half truths, and outright lies are being told during this political season just remember, *"to thine own self be true"* and stand, walk in, and vote in what you know and believe in the core of your being. That is one way that we can begin to heal the breach of trust that is taking place across the United States of America.

Life Lesson:
Home Is Where the Heart Is

The other day, I received a mass text from an acquaintance that is a contact in my cell phone asking for prayer at a certain time that particular day. I was at work when it came in, so by the time I read the text, it was past the time that they had requested the prayer. Since there were no details as to what to pray about I texted this person back and asked if there was some specific need that I could pray with them about. They replied back rather quickly and told me that their house was about to go into foreclosure and they did not know whether to fight it or not. They were at the beginning phase and did not know how to proceed; therefore they were seeking spiritual guidance. As I read the text, a flood of emotions hit me like a ton of cement bricks as I remembered the whole process that I had just gone through. The prevailing feeling of empathy flooded my heart as I thought about how two years ago I was at that place, wondering what I should do.

As we celebrate this Thanksgiving, they let us take time to be thankful for the things we have and the things we have lost. The reason why I say that is because often times we miss what is waiting to come into our lives because we are holding on to things that are no longer ours. While it is a hard process to let go, you must remember that it is some-

WHAT IS IT?

times even harder to hold on. In the case of the house that I lost, when I counted the cost of trying to keep it versus the cost of letting it go into foreclosure, it would have cost me more in terms of my inner peace and joy if I had tried to stay. Peace is wealth and worrying about how I was going to pay the mortgage when the money simply was not there, was just not worth it. I had friends who tried to convince me to sue the bank and Mortgage Company but I really did not feel the need to go that route. I felt like Job who said, "The Lord giveth and the Lord taketh away, blessed be the name of the Lord."

On the other side of it all, I am very thankful for having gone through that process because it forced me to get in touch with the real meaning of a home. My former house was functional in providing a stable place and shelter for me to raise my daughter through high school and into college. It was also there to protect and take care of my aging mother who stayed with me for seven years after my father passed away. It functioned as a treatment center for the occasional women that lived with us while they were in recovery, and it housed laughter, memories, tears, and holidays over the course of almost two decades. We made that house a home, and it served its purpose.

I realize today that home is where your heart is. Just as I packed up and moved out my furniture, television, refrigerator, clothes, and other tangible possessions; I also packed up my memories, tears, joy, pain, peace, love, hopes, and dreams, and I am now unpacking them to make the house that I am in now a home.

Life Lesson: Christmas, It's About Time

As I was growing up, I remember how my cousins, friends, and I could not wait until Christmas came. We like many children then and now would count down the time until Christmas would return, whether it was hours, days, or months away. Every time we thought of Christmas we got all excited and talked about what we wanted to receive. The main problem that we had was the fact that we had to wait and that wait was almost unbearable. It seemed like eternity until the blessed event of Christmas would finally make its way back around. Now it appears as though the years fly by and Christmas comes right after the Fourth of July! Whether you are ready or not it appears to come around with a bang. The retail stores and advertisers make sure that we know it is coming and what we need to buy in order to make it special.

As I thought about this the other day, I realized that it is all about time. Time is the great equalizer because we have the same amount of time each day. We all have twenty-four hours each day that we can use one way or the other. It's about time, and the way we focus our attention and prioritize our lives that determines whether we are making the most of what we have or wasting the precious little time that we have left. We can't "kill" time because time will outlive us all. When we have passed away, time will still be moving on.

So often we spend our lives wishing we were in another time. Whether it is the past or the future, the present is simply not good enough for us. I see this even in my granddaughter Tayla, who recently turned four-years old. She is already talking about how she cannot wait until she is old enough to lose her teeth like her older friends who are six and losing theirs. When she was two she talked of being three and when she became three she soon wanted to be a big girl of four. It is amazing how quickly we learn that to be the age we are now is simply not good enough.

It's about time and the sooner we learn that today is all we really have because tomorrow is gone and the future may never be, the happier we can be. Living in the present or the *now* as many are calling it can be discouraging if your present reality is not quite what you would like it to be. I believe that we can make the best of our time no matter what the circumstances are by making everyday like Christmas! We can recreate the good feelings and great anticipation and expectation that we had as children waiting to receive our presents on Christmas day by looking at each day as a present that we have just received. The only thing we have to do is unwrap it.

Three ways to maximize your Christmas this year:

1. Experience love, peace, and good cheer that are present during this season.
2. Pay particular attention to the good thoughts that emerge and write them down.
3. Remember to spread the goodness of Christmas to others who are going through tough times.

Life Lesson: What Do You Really Want?

Take thirty seconds and write down five things that you really want. Okay time is up. What do you have on your list? I asked this question during my latest life plan development seminar, and I received many answers. Some people stated that they wanted basic needs met such as food, shelter, clothing, and jobs, while others wanted social and emotional things like love, strong relationships, safety, security, peace, and happiness. However some people could not write anything down in thirty seconds because they simply didn't know what to write in such a short span of time.

WHAT IS IT?

What about you, do you know what you really want out of the life that you are currently living?

The answers to this question are tied to your purpose and destiny. The reason why you are here planted on earth. So many times we do not take time to listen to what is waiting to emerge from our hearts deep within. Therefore we go about our lives merely existing and not really living life to the fullest. The good thing is that once we become aware of the "itch that needs to be scratched" so to speak, we can then pursue our personal best in life.

May I submit to you that everyone needs a life plan no matter the age? A plan is simply a method for achieving an end that is oftentimes a detailed formulation of a program of action. I believe that the reasons only eight percent of people successfully achieve their New Year's resolutions are because number one their resolutions are not necessarily part of their life plan and number two, there are often times no real strategic plans developed to accomplish the desired outcomes. As the saying goes, if you fail to plan, then you plan to fail.

Before we can actually start developing our life plans, we must deal with five top obstacles that can hinder one's ability to act in life and not just react to life. These are definitely not all inclusive but if we successfully and strategically deal with each of the obstacles listed below we can confidently begin the process of developing our life plans.

Top Five Obstacles

1. Fear of the unknown
2. Inability to Focus
3. Forgetfulness of purpose
4. Fatigue that prevents action
5. Lack of Faithfulness that leads to procrastination

Life Lesson: Characteristics of a Healthy Life Plan

According to recent statistics, eighty percent of people never set goals for themselves.

A few months ago, I went through a very difficult time with a family whose mother had a stroke and had to be placed in the hospital. She continued to have mini strokes while she was in the hospital, and they had to eventually hook her up to life support. The machines were literally breathing for her and keeping her alive. This went on for several days and weeks. The doctors began to ask the family if they wanted to take her off of life support and see if she could breathe on her own. This was a very difficult decision for the family to make because she did not have a living

WHAT IS IT?

will. In the final analysis, they did give permission for her to be taken off of life support, and she died shortly thereafter. This reminded me of the Terri Schiavo case where a Florida woman was on life support from 1998–2005. Her husband Michael petitioned the court to remove her feeding tube. However, her parents were opposed and this resulted in a lengthy legal battle that included then US president, George W. Bush signing legislation to keep Terry Schiavo alive. After all attempts at appeals though the federal court system upheld the original decision to remove the feeding tube and they disconnected the feeding tube on March 18, 2005, and she died on March 31, 2005.

There has been tremendous education concerning the development of a living will over the past few decades to help families deal with situations that can occur when a loved one is rendered incapacitated and unable to make life and death decisions. A living will states your wishes regarding life support in the event that you are in a persistent vegetative state or irreversible coma and cannot communicate your wishes. After death, the living will can grant consent to an autopsy, bequeath anatomical gifts, and direct the disposition of your remains—whether you wish to be buried or cremated or neither.

While a living will is very important to have whenever you are unconscious; a life plan is very important to develop because it will help you to navigate through life while you are conscious. Developing a life plan is a lifelong process that begins from birth and continues throughout the span of your life. If it is such an important document to have, then why are there so few people willing to develop one? I heard one young lady say that she was taught to never plan for the future because you do not know what the future holds and therefore you cannot adequately plan. Whenever you are developing a life plan remember that you are not just planning for the future but navigating through the present that is leading to the future. Therefore, a life plan takes into account your past while living in your present and contemplating your future.

Five Characteristics of a Healthy Life Plan

1. Present-oriented
2. Action-oriented
3. Positive
4. Represents your life
5. Based upon your gifts and talents

Life Lesson: A Powerful Life Plan Must Include Divine Connections

WHAT IS IT?

Tarra and Bella was a very unlikely pair that lived at the Elephant Sanctuary in Tennessee until Bella's death in 2011. They were best friends that connected in a very unusual way. Although elephants are known to pair up two by two, it is most likely to be two elephants but not with Tarra and Bella. Tarra is an elephant but Bella was a stray dog who wandered onto the sanctuary grounds and found a soul mate in Tarra. Although the famous quote by John Donne is clearly about the connectivity of mankind it also applies to animals as well. No species are an island. We all need each other. Therefore, a solid life plan must be greater than one person's life alone. A powerful life plan must include divine connections. A life plan can only be accomplished through partnerships between those whose destinies are intertwined. Tarra and Bella's destinies were joined in order for them to accomplish the notoriety and greatness that were thrust upon them. Alone they were just another elephant and dog, but together they became a symbol of unity in diversity that will live past their time together.

So often we mistakenly develop life plans that are egocentric and centered just on our dreams and desires. What we must realize is that we need to include others in our life plans, not just as a way to get ahead but as a way of life. This can happen through divine connections that will facilitate our ability to accomplish our outcomes and goals in life. I say divine because they must be larger than life and deeper than the flesh. There must be heart-to-heart connections that will unlock the creativity needed to be successful. We often network and exchange business cards thinking that will somehow get us to where we need to be. However that is surface networking that may or may not lead to divine connections. Divine connections often happen unplanned by serendipity, so therefore we must always be prepared and open for what is waiting to emerge.

Keys to Unlocking Your Life Plan

- Be Present
- Be Authentic
- Stay Focused
- Pace Yourself
- Begin with the End in Mind

Life Lesson: Who Are You?

Mary was very outgoing and vibrant most of the time, however she began to feel isolated and alone whenever her children graduated high school and moved away to college. She felt as though she was no longer of any real value because her whole identity was tied up in her role as a single mother of two.

WHAT IS IT?

Tiffany was excited about finally getting a job after graduating college and looking for two years. The only problem was now that she had the job, she felt like a fish out of water. She had trouble sleeping at night and was always very self-conscious about whether she was doing the right thing or not.

At first Greg was on top of the world when he proposed to his fiancée of two years until he began to look at his old address book with names and numbers of women he had once dated. The reason he felt anxious was because Greg was known as a real "player" or ladies man.

These real-life case scenarios listed above all point to the same question that has to be answered at different stages of life and that is *who am I?* The reason why this is such a loaded question is because we often define ourselves based upon what we do or what roles we are currently playing in life without ever really knowing who we are at the essence of our being. The truth of the matter is we are all human beings not human doings. Therefore, you may be functioning in the roles of mother, student, or player, but that is not who you really are. Who you are is based upon your core values, character, and integrity. These are the things that make you no matter what roles you happen to be in. If you are not solidly aware of the essence of what makes you uniquely you, then you may experience confusion and anxiety when roles change.

Developing a life plan begins with answering the question, "Who am I?" The way you answer that will determine the goals and outcomes that you want to achieve in life. For instance if you say currently I am functioning in the roles of mother, account executive, author, and volunteer at a homeless shelter; you will need to write a life plan for each of those roles with the specifics of what, how, and when included. On a deeper level, you will also need to answer the question who you are as it relates to my purpose and destiny on planet earth. Someone once said that we are spirits having a human experience. What does that mean to you and what kind of experience do you desire to have no matter what roles you are currently fulfilling in life?

Exercise to help you develop your life plan from within,

I Am

I Desire

I Will

I Love

I Need

I Want

I Have

Life Lesson: Three Things I Learned as a Toddler

When I was a toddler, I was very petite and I did not drink much milk. I also cried a lot for no apparent reason as well, maybe because I was hungry. I am told and I also have vague recollections of the following event that occurred when I was around eighteen-months old. My cousin who was the same age as I was considered a *greedy* child because he consumed all his milk, and then he would snatch my bottle which was always full and drink it all down. I would cry and run away from him. One day, he came over with his mom, and we were in the front room drinking our bottles, and he finished his and looked at me. I knew what he was going to try to do, and I ran away from him. A chase ensued and he backed me into a corner and tried to grab my bottle of milk. I, having nowhere else to run, did something different this time. Instead of giving him my bottle and crying, I begin to swing my arms really fast and hit him on the head. At that point, he dropped his bottle and ran in the other direction crying and screaming. I was told that he never tried to take my bottle of milk again.

I learned three major lessons from this experience early in life that have stuck with me over many years and through major life events.

1. I learned the importance of facing my fears and having courage. Fear is a natural emotion and a major part of life no matter what the age. When we turn around and face the things that are chasing us, we may be surprised to realize that they are not as bad as they seem.

2. I learned to become a fighter. Unfortunately during my early years in school, I found myself literally fighting children who would come up against me. I would always have crowds of children following me home shouting "fight, fight, fight," because they knew I was going to be having it out with someone. As I matured though, I learned that there are much better ways to fight than to fight them with your fists. I became a lover who fights through non-violence like the late great Dr. Martin Luther King, Jr.

Today when I am backed into a corner I still come out swinging but not with my fists but with my faith.

3. I learned the importance of holding on to what is mine. Over the years, I have been amazed at the number of people who see something that you have, and they want and think it is okay to try and take it from you. The things that truly belong to us are not material things but the things that make us who we are like, love, integrity, faith, and hope. Unfortunately some people will even try to steal that. That is when I have to put my spiritual dukes up and *fight the good fight of faith*.

Life Lesson: Things I Learned as Founder of Mothers In Crisis

Several years ago, I went to pick up a woman for a drug and alcohol support group meeting that I facilitated in a rural county in Florida. When she and her children got in the van, she sat in the front seat on the right side. Upon pulling off, I looked in the mirror and noticed that her left hand was balled up tightly in a fist. I asked her whether she was okay and what did she have in her hand? She opened it up and there was a "stem"—drug paraphernalia for smoking crack-cocaine—still smoking from recent use. I was stunned and appalled and my immediate reaction was to ask her to get off of the van. However as I began to speak my anger subsided as I looked into the very somber brown eyes of her five children. I lowered my voice and asked her what she wanted to do. I told her it was her choice and if she really wanted help she could still come to the meeting. She gave me the stem and held her head down in defeat and shame and whispered a plea for help. I immediately disposed of the stem and proceeded to drive to the group meeting with streams of tears running down my face.

I started Mothers In Crisis (MIC), a non-profit organization comprised of women in recovery from drugs and alcohol addiction, in 1991 during the crack-cocaine epidemic that was plaguing communities around the nation. It reached both urban and rural communities throughout the state of Florida. Women who were once the backbone of many single-parent families were now strung out on drugs, leaving their children to be cared for by relatives or the state. I had four years clean and had been working as a social worker for non-profit drug treatment programs for three years when I founded MIC. We did great work and impacted the lives of thousands of families over the past two decades. I was forced to retire as executive director and pursue other endeavors whenever Mothers In Crisis lost most of its funding due to the economic downturn that the nation has been experiencing these past five years. Now,

WHAT IS IT?

Mothers In Crisis is a volunteer organization that is currently implementing the *Young Sisters In Success Mentoring Program* and other initiatives.

Several weeks ago, I was watching the news and I saw Attorney General Pam Bondi speaking about the "Statewide Task Force on Prescription Drug Abuse & Newborns Final Report." I experienced a deep sigh as well as butterflies in my stomach as I listened and realized that two decades later that we are still trying to protect our most vulnerable citizens from the harmful effects of drug addiction. I immediately contacted the Attorney General's office to get a copy of the report and offer my experience and expertise.

As I read the report, I realized that three components that we believe in and that have helped us to be successful through Mothers In Crisis are found prominently throughout the recommendations of the task force and those are: *prevention*, *intervention*, and *treatment*. No matter what the drug of choice may be, drug education and awareness must be a key ingredient in helping to combat this growing problem. Knowledge is power and while strategies may change the message remains the same, "Drug Steal and Violence Kills so don't use drugs or use your fist but use your brain and remember this, drugs steal and violence kills!"

Life Lesson: The Force of Hope

Where Is Hope? Hope is found in the Breath that I Breathe;

In the Stars in the Sky and in the Cool of the Breeze.

Hope is found in a Baby's Cry; or Tears rolling down the Eye,

Of one who knows that every good thing Flows from the Heart of God.

Hope is found in the Birds that Sing, in the Grass as it Grows, In the Smell of a Rose, in the Dew as it settles upon the Ground.

Hope can be found in the middle of Pain, in the Streets of Frustration,

And in the Home of the Name that is above every Name!

Hope is found when you Hear the Name, Think the Name, or Say the Name,

It's all the Same.

Because, Jesus is hope.

> This poem is taken from my book,
> *As Long As There Is Breath In Your Body,*
> *There Is Hope.*

WHAT IS IT?

Hope is one of the most powerful forces in the whole entire world. Through hope lives, families, communities, and nations are changed; but without it entire generations can be destroyed. Hope is that thing that keeps you moving towards your goal even when you can't see it. I wrote in my first book, *As Long As There Is Breath In Your Body, There Is Hope*, that hope is like lights in the midst of a dark tunnel that shows you the way as you walk through dark places along life's journey.

If hope is so powerful then why is that we often feel as though we are hopeless to bring about change in the world? Could it possibly be because of all the negativity that exists; or perhaps it is because of past attempts that have failed? The other day as I was watching the HBO television series *Enlightened* and catching up on all of the episodes something that was said really moved me. In the latest show, the main character's ex-husband said to her that *she just had too much hope for this world*. I said, "Wow that is a mouthful!" Why did I say that? Because I believe that hopeful people are often seen as naive or idealistic and not rational or realistic. But I beg to differ, I believe hope-filled people are the ones who are realistic because in reality it is going to take continual hope to live positively in this world.

With so much doom and gloom looming from the government and other dismal forecasts, it is easy to become cynical and fearful. We must keep hope alive by focusing on the good and not the bad. There are always good things to anticipate like life, health, love, etc. just waiting in the wings to be embraced. You see hope is for the future so no matter how tough it is right now picture tomorrow through the lens of hope and see things the way you desire them to be and not as others may say they will be. If this seems a little too simple and naive to you, just think of the alternative. You can live your life experiencing hard and difficult times now while thinking of the even tougher times that you will experience later. Now that doesn't make you feel warm and fuzzy all over, does it? Of course not because thoughts like that can bring you down and allow hopelessness to swallow you up like fog rolling over a lake.

The whole point of my poem "Where Is Hope" is that hope can be found in everything we just have to look for it. Remember, *As Long As There Is Breath In Your Body, There Is Hope*. May the force of hope be with you!

Life Lesson: "Weebles Wobble but They Don't Fall Down"

I grabbed the wind in the palm of my hand. I made a fist and held it real tight; I kept it that way for most of the night. Curiosity got the best of me and I decided to take a peek and see what the wind looked like as it sat in my hand. I opened my hand very slowly, one finger at a time; I looked for the wind

Life Lesson: Power Struggles

Lauren came home an emotional wreck once again after struggling with a co-worker. This was increasingly common in the past several months ever since she became the target of one of her supervisors. It seemed like nothing she did was right, and she had to hear about it in staff meetings in front of everybody. As a result, she began to be moody and short with those around her at work and home. She did little things at work to let her supervisor know that she was not pleased, like wearing a frown, not speaking, and generally isolating herself. She started losing confidence in her level of competence, and therefore she became very defensive. She found herself always trying to justify something she said or did both at work and at home.

When "Lauren," not her real name, shared with me what she was going through at work I listened as a good friend and I did not say much. I empathized with her because I had faced similar situations in my life. I needed her to know that I was hearing her and that I was on her side because she really needed a friend. After she vented through laughter and tears, I asked her if I could ask her a few questions. She had finally let her defenses down and felt safe so she said, "Sure." The first question that I asked was, "Who has the power?" She looked at me for a while and finally said, "Excuse me?" I laughed and asked the question again this way, "Who are you fighting with?" At that point she just looked at me strangely waiting and I said, "Think about it."

Finally after a long pause which would probably be uncomfortable for most people she said, "I have been giving my power away." "Bingo!" I said.

What Lauren was engaged in is a typical power struggle that we often see magnified in parent-child relationships; but truth be told we engage in them well beyond our youth and in multiple relationships. I define power struggles as, "…those places defined by one person trying to get another person to do something in their way, idea, or methodology. It is often seen in children and parents and it can lead to some very unhealthy exchanges. These are situations where either the parent or the child is trying to get their way and neither one wants to back down or compromise." I go on to say, "The same thing applies in other relationships where there are power struggles. When you realize your position or place you can develop true strategies to get your desired outcomes without declaring war and fighting for a position that either, A. You already have, or B. You don't truly have the authority to make the call. It is always better to *chill* and not react… That takes emotional maturity which requires growth and transformation.

When Lauren realized that she was engaged in a power struggle and thus giving away her true power as the competent, highly qualified professional that she is; she decided to step back and come up with real strategies that will bring about true progress and peace.

WHAT IS IT?

Life Lesson: A Mother's Love

A Mother's love is sent from above;
Created by God to show how it's done;
It nurtures, it heals, it covers, and it fills;
It possesses and caresses;
Just like the One and Only Begotten Son.
It is unconditional love that is sent from above,
From God our Father who is also a mother.
The closest thing that I have ever seen;
To the real deal of love that is like none other,
Is manifested in God in the person of a Mother

> This poem is taken from my book,
> *You Are Beautiful*, and it was written years ago
> especially for my mother the late Louise Clark.

I wrote this poem for my mother because like many people, I found my mother to be an extraordinary woman. I owe her my life. I don't say that just because she gave birth to me. Yes, I appreciate that but what I am referring to is the time when I was caught up in the vicious cycle of addiction for twelve years of my life and how it was my mother who stuck by me and prayed for me.

I really wish my mother could have stayed around a little longer in order to read *You Are Beautiful* not just because of the poem included and the fact that I dedicated it to her.

I believe the book would have really been a blessing to my mother because she always struggled with her perception of how she looked. She was a beautiful woman even at the age of eighty-five. Perfect strangers would tell her how pretty she looked and they always complimented her on her smile. The thing that struck me was that she would come home and tell the stories of how she was praised for her looks by someone and then say something like, "I don't know why they said that" or "They were just saying something." When she said things like that I would gently rebuke her and say, "They said it because it's true." She would then smile but I knew deep down she didn't believe that she was beautiful or deserving of the compliments. You see my mother was from the Deep South. She grew up in a small town in North Florida (Freeport), and then she moved even deeper south to the Mississippi Delta. Her grandfather was a slave, and she grew up in that era where people believed that "white was right" but "black get back." They had such things as the paper bag test, if you were darker than a paper bag, then you were considered too dark. Many black women including my mother grew up with a self-loathing that in many cases they passed down to their children, especially the girls. I wasn't affirmed as a beautiful child because I was darker than the rest of my siblings and my hair was quite kinky growing up, and on top of that I was tender-headed.

WHAT IS IT?

Life Lesson: I Believe I Can Fly

I love to rollerblade on the St. Mark's trail whenever the weather permits. It's like flying for me because of the freedom that I feel just skating along. Sometimes I listen to music on my mp3 player while other times I just listen to the sounds of nature, which I equate with the sounds of freedom. Hearing the birds sing their melodic chirps, the crickets playing their orchestra of sounds, and the low croaks of the frogs, all seem to denote a harmony that is from another world.

The last time that I went skating I decided to imagine that I could actually fly, and I thought about where I would go if I could go anywhere in the world right now. I thought about Hawaii and the Caribbean Islands, and I imagined myself flying over the beautiful oceans of both places, but I did not stop and settle in those places in my mind because I felt a tugging and pulling to another destination. As I skated along the trail in my mind's eye, I saw myself headed to Bangladesh. Immediately my flow of imagination was interrupted, and I began to ask myself why in the world would I want to go to Bangladesh? I wasn't quite sure where it was but I was certain that I didn't speak the language. After a while, I decided to stop fighting my imagination of going to Bangladesh and just play it out in my mind. I took up flight again in my imagination, and I went to Bangladesh and hovered over the Rana Plaza on the outskirts of Dhaka where the garment factory collapsed on April 24, killing over a thousand people. I quickly swooped down and landed in the midst of a crowd of people screaming and crying. Although their language was Bengali, their pain was easily understood. At this point I stopped skating and stepped to the side on the trail and cried. I cried for the thousands of workers primarily women who were poor and just trying to make a living working in adverse conditions for very little pay. After crying, I prayed for strength for the country and true change to take place so that this could never happen again. I wiped my tears away and started skating again. This time I turned my music on and decided to stay on the ground.

Later that day, I thought again about why of all the places in the world that I could imagine myself flying to, I would pick Bangladesh and experience such sadness? I could have imagined going to the mountains or the oceans of the world and experienced great peace and relaxation. After a while, it came to me that pain is meant to be shared and while I could not go to Bangladesh in my physical body, my heart could go there. I had listened to the news about what happened when the garment factory collapsed in the sound bites of reporting, but it wasn't until I placed myself in Bangladesh that I really got it. I really felt the pain and was moved to follow the story and see where I can help. I guess my next imaginary flight will be to Oklahoma.

WHAT IS IT?

Life Lesson:
The Beauty of Laughter

I believe that a good sense of humor is vitally important in order to keep your sanity especially today with so much upheaval and turmoil in the world. That is why it is very important to look for the absurd in everyday living. With that in mind, I will share an event that happened to a friend of mine. Mary, not her real name, was at a church program that had reached a feverish pitch during the praise and worship portion of the service. Mary began to dance in the aisle as she sang. She raised her hands and shook her head to the music so hard until her wig that was attached to her hair fell right off her head. At that moment, those who saw her gasped and looked stunned wondering what Mary was going to do next. To everyone's surprise, she picked up her wig, swung it around, and kept on dancing. That gave everyone permission to laugh with her not at her, and that is the important thing when we think of the power of laughter. Laughter at others produces hurt feelings and isolation while laughter with others produces joy and community.

> A good sense of humor will make up for bad hair days, pimples, and bloating, that is, if you don't take yourself too seriously. When you don't look or feel your best, look for the humor in your situation. Sometimes, just looking in the mirror and see-

ing how silly you look will cause you to laugh at yourself!

> This excerpt is taken from my book, *You Are Beautiful*.

Laughing at yourself will help to take the edge off of some tough situations but in order to do that you must have a healthy self-worth. You must know how valuable you are and in spite of whatever the circumstances are that you are facing, they do not define your worth. In the above example with Mary, it was obvious that at the moment that her wig fell off, she was not concerned about others and their opinions. When you free yourself from the fear of what others think, feel, and say about you, you can begin to laugh at yourself with greater abandonment.

Five Ways to Develop a Good Sense of Humor:

1. Know your value and free yourself from the opinions of others
2. Laugh with others
3. Respect others
4. Don't be afraid to laugh out loud
5. Look for the ridiculous in everyday situations

6. The most important thing that one can do in order to remain beautiful is to laugh

Life Lesson: The Success of Being

I participated in a panel discussion that consisted of a diverse group of primarily ministers talking about success while answering the question, "does gifting and anointing guarantee success?" Well as you can imagine this was a loaded topic that could be looked at from many different angles. I came prepared with my books, *You Are Beautiful*, *Rare Anointing*, and *As Long As There Is Breath In Your Body, There Is Hope* and was ready to discuss various points including the definitions of gifting and anointing. I was also ready to talk about success as it relates to purpose and destiny because it is at the forefront of my mind as I am finishing up my latest book.. So you might say I was ready or so I thought. What started out as a typical panel discussion quickly morphed into a format mirroring, *The View*, and I was like Whoopi Goldberg as I found myself making jokes while opinions were flying. I couldn't really get serious because I was sandwiched on a couch that made me look like a pickle between the meat and the bun.

As I continued to ponder the topic days after the panel discussion, I thought about the success of being. So many times we are so busy caught up in doing and having until the simple act of being gets lost. When you first meet someone, the second question that they normally ask after asking your name is usually, "What do you do?" We then begin to list the occupations and roles that we possess and impress with our success and accomplishments. That is all well and good but what about who you are as it relates to being and becoming. After all, as I always say, we are human beings not human doings.

The success of being is actually realizing that success is a state of being. Just showing up and contributing what you can, when you can, in the way that you can, is success because not everyone can show up and be present in their lives and especially in the lives of others. My PR coach, Pam Perry, always says, "Those that show up, go up." That is so true. We must show up in life through the good times and the bad. We cannot check out or give up on our dreams and goals for life. When we show up for life, we are destined to be successful at being who we are called to be. Just being you is a success because no one can beat you at being you, though believe me, some may try.

No matter what gifts or talents that you may have, just remember that they are there for you to present and be present to the assignments at hand. Take it one day at a time, and the things that are supposed to open up to you, will.

WHAT IS IT?

Three Ways to be Successful at Being Human

1. Know who you are
2. Cultivate your gifts and talents
3. Show up

Dream Again

I had a dream last night but it didn't last long;
In the dream I was singing a song,
About how in life things can go wrong;
But even then there is a chance to go on.

I had a dream last night about what love looked like
And in the dream I thought about the plight of men and women
Caught up in a daze, purple haze, eyes all glazed, looking half crazed,
Walking and wandering through life un-phased by all of the chaos and sin all around, looking for love in a world turned upside down.

I had a dream last night but something had changed
The tables had turned and inside my head burned with the awareness and knowledge that life is for living and love is for loving and songs are for singing and in the midst of it all my alarm clock started ringing.
I arose from my bed, shook my head, and thought about the things that I had reaped, and then it dawned on me that I wasn't really asleep!

WHAT IS IT?

For the first time in my life my eyes were wide opened and I was aware and awake to the things that make life worth living and time worth giving to the things that bring release and offer peace.

So whether awake or asleep, dream of a life filled with songs for the soul and love that makes whole whatever is broken.
Dream of hope and joy for better days ahead;
And when you dream get out of your bed and bring to reality the things that were said!

Bibliography

Tompkins, Rosalind. *As Long As There Is Breath In Your Body, There Is Hope*, Lake Mary, Florida: Creation House, A Strang Company, 2005

———. *You Are Beautiful*, Durham, Conneticut: Strategic Book Publishing, 2010

Tompkins-Whiteside, Rosalind. *Rare Anointing*, Lake Mary, Florida: Creation House, A Strang Company, 2007